The World's Harvest

COAL

Jacqueline Dineen

Missouri Western State College
Hearnes Learning Resources Center
4525 Downs Drive
St. Joseph, Missouri 64507

ENSLOW PUBLISHERS, INC.
Bloy St & Ramsey Ave.
Box 777
Hillside, N.J. 07205

The story of how nature made coal, geologists find it, miners dig for it, and people use it, all over the world.

The picture above shows a dragline bucket in use at Peak Downs opencast mine, Queensland
[*cover*] *The cover picture shows a 'road-header' boring a tunnel through to a Yorkshire coalface*
[*title page*] *The picture on the title page shows a dredger cutting coal at Morwell opencast mine in Victoria*
[*1–24*] *All other pictures are identified by number in the text*

Contents

	Introduction	3
1.	What is coal?	5
2.	Finding the coal	11
3.	Starting a coal mine	14
4.	Working at a longwall mine	21
5.	Other methods of mining	25
6.	How coal is used	29
	Index	32

This series was developed for a worldwide market.

First American Edition, 1988
© Copyright 1985 Young Library Ltd
All rights reserved.
No part of this book may be reproduced by any means without the written permission of the publisher.

Printed in the United States of America

10 9 8 7 6 5 4 3 2 1

LIBRARY OF CONGRESS
Library of Congress Cataloging-in-Publication Data

Dineen, Jacqueline.
    Coal / Jacqueline Dineen.
        p.   cm. -- (The World's harvest)
    Includes index.
    Summary: Explains how this important fuel is created, found, and mined.
    ISBN 0-89490-212-1
    1. Coal--Juvenile literature. [1. Coal.] I. Title.
 II. Series: Dineen, Jacqueline. World's harvest.
 TP325.D56 1988
 553.2'4--dc19   88-1184
                                                                 CIP
                                                                  AC

Introduction

Coal is one of our most important natural fuels. Like oil and gas, it is found under the earth or the sea. Unlike oil and gas, however, it cannot be brought to the surface by pipeline. Men like the miner in picture [1] have to go down into the earth to cut it out of the rock. What is coal and why is it so valuable to us?

In chapter 1 I tell you how coal was formed millions of years ago, and how it came to be buried deep in the ground. I describe the different types of coal, and explain how people

[1]

first discovered that it was there.

Finding coal is a complicated business, and I tell you something about this in chapter 2. I explain the work of the geologists who study the rocks underground and find places where they think coal might be buried. I tell you about seismic surveys, which are often used to locate a coal seam, and how test drillings are made for rock samples. Then we see how mining companies are trying to find coal at sea, and bring coal out from beneath shallow waters.

In chapter 3, I describe how a coal mine is set up so that it runs safely and efficiently. These days, modern machinery and equipment are used, and computers monitor what is going on underground. Working underground is far safer than it used to be in the early days of mining. You will see what a modern mine consists of, on the surface and underground.

In chapter 4, we go underground with a miner who is working at the coalface. I tell you how he prepares for his work, how he gets to the coalface, and what work he does when he gets there.

In chapter 5 I describe some of the other types of mining which are used in different parts of the world. Opencast mines and drift (slope) mines are for coal which is fairly near the surface. Modern room-and-pillar mines and retreat mines are versions of the deep underground mines described in earlier chapters.

Finally, I talk about some of the ways in which coal is used in our modern world, and from this you will see what a vital fuel it is.

1 · *What is coal?*

A piece of coal looks like black rock. Yet when you put coal on the fire it burns. If you put rock on the fire, it would not burn. So what is coal?

Coal is found in layers (called 'seams') deep in the earth. These seams of coal are sandwiched between layers of rock. Picture [2] shows what these rock layers look like. When coal miners are digging out the coal, they sometimes find prints of leaves and bits of woodbark. They may also find leaf fossils, like the one in picture [3]. These marks give the biggest clue to what coal really is.

The story of coal begins about 350 million years ago, long before there were any people on the earth. The earth's crust was still changing shape, and forming continents and seas. Parts of the earth's surface were covered with swamps and lakes. Rivers flowed into these waterlogged areas, bringing mud and sand with them. Huge trees and giant ferns grew up all over the swamps, forming large forests. As the centuries passed, these forests became very dense. When the trees died they fell into the swamp, where they rotted down and changed into peat.

The rivers poured more water and silt into the swamp, and the peat was buried under layers of sand and mud. More vegetation grew up, died, and was buried. The process continued for millions and millions of years. As the layers of peat were buried deeper and

[2]

Peat is a compressed layer of decayed vegetation which lies on the surface of the earth. It is the first stage of coal formation, and can itself be used as a fuel.

deeper, the silt that covered them was pressed down more and more tightly. At last it was compressed so much that it formed layers of rock. The peat also was compressed, and changed by heat and bacteria, into what we now know as coal.

Coal is formed only in these swampy conditions. They lasted for about 80 million years. Eventually they ended as the earth's crust began to settle down. More and more layers of rock were formed on top of the coal, but no more vegetation was buried with them. By the time the continents had formed into the shapes they have today, the layers of coal were buried. Sometimes they are still quite near the surface, but they are also found hundreds or even thousands of metres underground.

Coal is made of carbon, hydrogen, and oxygen. Carbon is what makes coal burn so well. The deeper the coal is buried, the more hydrogen and oxygen is squeezed out. This leaves a coal which is nearly all carbon.

[4]

Peat will not change into true coal unless it is buried under a great weight of rock, so that it is compressed. It will change at first (after many millions of years) into a brown, crumbly type of coal called lignite. This is the softest type of coal, and it does not burn so well as other sorts. Lignite is normally found in rocks which were formed towards the end of the coal-bearing period. Therefore it is usually found nearer the surface than other types of coal. There are large quantities of lignite around the world. Seams of lignite in Australia are often 65 metres thick, and there is one which is more than 250 metres thick. You can see how thick the one in picture [4] is, but you can also see that it is not very far below the surface.

When lignite was buried under more layers of rock, it changed to bituminous coal. This is the most common type of coal. It is black, and is formed in layers. It may be bright and shiny, or dull and sooty, or something in between.

Another type of coal sometimes found at the same level as bituminous coal is 'cannel'. Cannel is harder and more brittle. It has no layers, and is a dull black. Cannel burns with a long flame, like a candle's (which is probably how it got its name).

If bituminous coal is buried even deeper, the extra heat and pressure change it into a very hard coal called anthracite. Anthracite is nearly all carbon, and has a dullish shine.

Early discoveries of coal

People have been burning coal for thousands of years. But if coal is buried so deep in the ground, how did primitive people first discover that it was there? The answer is quite simple.

Although most coal is buried under layers of rock, some is found near the surface too. The movement of the earth's crust, and disturbances such as earthquakes and volcanoes, shifted the layers of rock about. Some rocks containing coal were pushed upwards, and exposed on rock faces such as cliffs and hillsides. You can see an example of this in picture [5].

Coal seams on or near the surface are called outcrops. People probably discovered coal by accident when they built a fire on one of these outcrops. Once the discovery had been made, they began to search for coal along the banks of streams or on the sides of cliffs.

They realised that the coal they could see was the end of a seam which disappeared into the earth. So they dug tunnels to get it out. The tunnels into the hillsides soon collapsed, so the people moved on to find another outcrop. Gradually they noticed a pattern in these outcrops. They worked out how the seams ran beneath the surface. Then they began to dig from above, making a vertical shaft for the miners to climb down to the seam. Nowadays, coal deep in the earth is found by a complicated system of surveys. I will tell you about surveys in the next chapter.

[5]

At the moment we are taking 3 billion tonnes of coal out of the earth each year. More than one-fifth of that comes from the United States, and almost as much is found in Russia and in China. Other big coal producers are Australia, Britain, Germany, and Poland.

[6]   Coal is a vitally important fuel to us today. In picture [6] you can see a typical power station, with its vast coal stocks. To produce electricity, power stations burn millions of tonnes of coal during the year. Industries such as steel works could not operate without it.

The trouble is that—although the coal has lain there for so many millions of years—we do not know exactly where it all is. The coal we know about may only be enough to last another 200 or 300 years. This is why the search for coal continues. We hope we can find new coalfields on land, and under the sea. Perhaps we can also use some of the seams which people gave up on years ago, now that we have better equipment and safer methods.

2 · Finding the coal

It is easy enough to find coal on or near the surface. To find coal deep in the ground is more difficult. When a mining company is looking for coal, the first person it turns to is a geologist. Geologists are people who study the earth's crust and its rock formations. They can find the type of rocks which are likely to contain coal.

One way of finding out about rocks below the surface is to conduct a seismic survey. The geologists in picture [7] are studying a print-out of a seismic survey. Shallow holes are drilled in the ground and filled with explosives. When the explosives are set off, the shock waves travel down through the layers of rock. Then they bounce back to the surface, where

[7]

they are picked up by microphones. These sound waves are affected by the density of the rocks they pass through. By noting the time it takes the sound waves to travel back to the surface, the geologist can tell what sort of rocks there are. He can also tell if there is likely to be a coal seam.

When the geologists have found an area which they think contains coal, the mining company makes a test drilling. First, a drilling rig is set up. A hollow drill pipe is rotated into the ground, and the drill bores its way down into the rock. New sections of pipe are added so that the drill goes deeper and deeper. From time to time, the drill pipe is pulled out. Inside the hollow tube is a length of rock showing all the different layers. This is called a 'core'. Picture [8] shows the core being taken out of the pipe. If the drill pipe reaches coal, the geologists can see how thick the seam is and how deep underground it lies. They decide whether the coal looks worth mining. If it does, they make more test drillings to find out how big the coalfield is, and how many seams there are.

Coal seams were formed before the seas and continents had settled down to their present shape. Many coal seams were later covered by sea. These huge reserves of coal under the sea are now being mined in fairly shallow waters near the coast. The mine entrance is on land, but the tunnels run down and along under the sea-bed. So far, people have not found a way of mining for coal in the middle of the oceans.

Seismic surveys are made at sea from ships. Explosions are set off from one ship, and the

[8]

sound waves are picked up and monitored by another ship. When coal is found, test drillings are made to find out what the seams are like.

Drilling rigs are set up at sea, just as they are for oil and gas production. In shallow waters up to about 30 metres deep, a fixed platform is used. The drill pipe travels nearly a kilometre into the seabed to bring up core samples.

A drill ship like the one in picture [9] can find coal in deeper waters. It is like an ordinary ship except that it has a derrick on the deck. The drill pipe passes from the derrick down through the hull. Drill ships sail about, making test drillings. A problem with them used to be that they could be buffeted around by wind or stormy seas, making it impossible to drill properly. Nowadays, computers monitor weather conditions very carefully, and also steer the ship automatically.

From their work near the shores, geologists are sure that there are billions of tonnes of coal under the sea further out. Perhaps one day we will find a way of getting at it.

[9]

3 · Starting a coal mine

Coal mining today is very different from the early mining I told you about in chapter 1. Some of those simple mines were called 'bell pits', because they were shaped rather like a bell, as you can see in picture [10]. The coal was hauled to the surface in buckets like water from a well. The main problem with bell pits was that they used to cave in as the miners dug further into the coal seam. To get at more coal, they had to prop up the roof of the mine in some way.

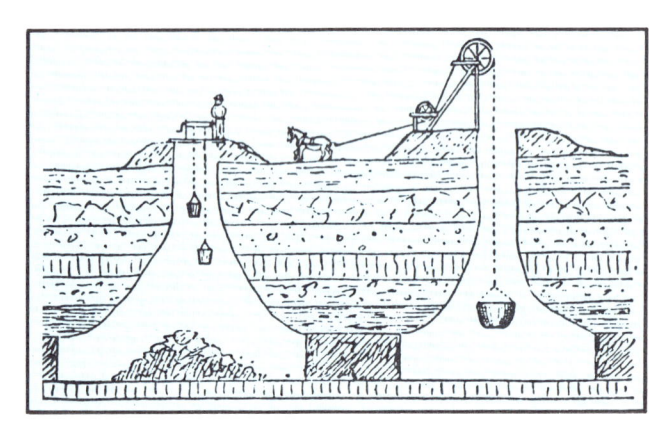

[10]

The next type of mine was the room-and-pillar which you can see in picture [11]. It started off like a bell pit, but was dug into a square space to form a room. A pillar of coal was left in place to hold up the roof, and another room was dug next to the first. More and more rooms were dug, and pillars left in place, until the coal seam looked a bit like a chessboard.

Room-and-pillar mines were used for a long time, and they still are in the United States. They had one big disadvantage, however. Can you think what this was? The roof was held up by coal. The mining companies wanted to get all the coal out of the ground, not leave half of it behind in the mine. The obvious solution was to find something else to prop up the tunnels.

The next idea was the one still used today—'longwall' mining. It is called 'longwall' because all the coal is taken off a long, continuous wall.

A shaft was cut down to the coal seam. Tunnels were driven into the seam to expose

[12]

A coalface is the end of a coal seam being cut at the moment. As cutting continues, the coalface moves back along the seam. You only get a coalface in longwall mining or retreat mining.

the 'coalface'. As the miners cut the coal, they built timber supports to hold the roof up.

Thirty years ago, miners went down the mine with picks and shovels and cut the coal by hand. Pit ponies hauled tubs of coal along the underground roads. The work was dirty, dark, and dangerous. There were cave-ins and rockfalls which could kill miners working underground. There was danger from flooding as water seeped through the rocks. The methane gas found in coal mines caused explosions. Today nearly all coal is cut by machine, and much of the underground work is monitored or controlled by computers at the surface. It is still dirty and dark down a mine, but it is safer than it used to be.

Cutting coal is only one of the tasks of a coal mine. The coal has to be brought to the surface, stored, washed, graded, and delivered to the customer. So how is a modern coal mine set up and organized to be safe and efficient?

[13]

The first step is to 'sink' (cut) vertical shafts from the surface to the coal. You can see a shaft being sunk in picture [12]. Coal can be mined at a depth of five kilometres or more. There may be several seams in the same coalfield. A mine has at least two shafts so that fresh air may be circulated underground. Powerful fans on the surface draw fresh air down the 'downcast' shaft and stale air up the 'upcast' shaft. These shafts are also used for lowering men and equipment to the coal seams.

A network of tunnels leads from the bottom of the shafts to the coalfaces. These tunnels are bored by the sort of machine in our cover picture. The roof is not supported by timber props these days. In the modern longwall mine, steel arches are used instead.

Alternatively, in some American mines they use a system called 'roof bolting'. Picture [13] shows a machine driving metal bolts, five or six

A coalfield is the whole area containing coal seams being mined. A coalfield often contains several mines.

metres long, up into the roof of the tunnel. Like a giant plug it holds the strata firmly in place.

A well established mine is like a big underground town. There are offices and workshops near the bottom of the shaft. The coalfaces being worked may be several kilometres from the shafts, so the miners are carried to their work on trains.

The workers on the surface

On the surface there are several buildings. Some are for the miners and other workers, and some are for the coal when it arrives from the mine. The miners need somewhere to clean up and change their clothes after work. There is a canteen where they can have a meal. There are offices for surface workers who see to the running of the mine. In the surface control room, computers monitor what is happening underground, and control some operations automatically. Controllers at the surface can telephone down to miners at the coalface. In the shafts there are lifts called 'cages'. They carry the miners down to the coal, and bring them up again at the end of their shift. The coal is brought to the surface in large containers called skips. The cages and skips are hauled up and down by winding gear at the top of the shafts. In picture [14] you can see the derrick containing the winding gear. It is a familiar sight at every vertical shaft mine.

When the coal gets to the surface it is still in a rough state, mixed with bits of rock and dirt. It is taken to the preparation plant. There it is

[14]

[15] sorted by machines to remove these bits and pieces. Finally it is loaded on to coal trains.

Picture [15] gives an overall view of the surface of a mine. The coal tips are on the far left. Just behind are the railway tracks. The two bulky towers contain the winding gear. Most of the buildings in between the towers and the railway tracks are part of the preparation plant.

A coal mine can be worked for years and years before all the coal has been cut and brought to the surface. By that time the underground tunnels may cover 300 square kilometres. In the next chapter I tell you what happens in this dark, dirty, and mysterious world deep in the earth.

4 · *Working at a longwall mine*

Coal mines are not all run in exactly the same way. A mine may be set up and run by a private mining company, as in the United States, or by a national authority as in Britain. There will be different rules and methods of working. There are also different types of mines, which I tell you about in the next chapter. But now I will tell you something about a miner's work in a fairly typical modern longwall mine.

Miners often work on a shift system. Instead of everyone working the same hours each day, there are three or four teams of workers. As one team finishes, a new shift starts. A shift system keeps the mine operating day and night.

When a miner arrives for work, the first thing he does is to change out of his ordinary clothes into his working clothes. This includes a helmet to protect his head from rockfalls and from bumps on the low ceilings. There are also overalls, kneepads, gloves, and stout boots with steel toecaps to protect his feet. He collects his battery-operated lamp to clip on to his helmet, which you can see in several pictures in this book. He also carries a special mask to protect him from poisonous gases if there should be a fire or an explosion.

Before he goes underground, the miner is

Safety down the mine

given two numbered discs. This is a safety precaution. He hands one disc in as he goes into the cage at the top of the shaft. He hands the second one in when he comes back to the surface after his shift. By this method the surface workers know who is underground. They can raise the alarm if there are any discs missing at the end of the shift.

No one is allowed to carry cigarettes or matches down the mine, because the methane gas could cause a fire or explosion. Before the miner goes into the cage he is searched, in case he has forgotten this important rule.

The cage holds up to thirty miners at a time. The cage travels very fast, and in no time the miner is at the bottom, ready to start work. The foreman in charge of the team tells each man where he is working for that shift. The miner sets off for the coalface. The main roadway at the bottom of the shaft is brightly lit, so he does not need his helmet lamp yet. He waits for the diesel train, like the one in picture [16], that will take him to the coalface. Some coal mines have conveyor belts on which the man sits to be carried along.

The train takes the miner along the main roadways, but he has to walk the last few hundred metres to the coalface. There is no lighting in the tunnel now, so he only has his helmet lamp to see by. He may have to crawl the last few metres to the point where he is to start work, if the roof is very low.

Just think about this for a moment. There is the miner in the depths of the earth. Five kilometres above his head rivers are flowing. Thousands of people are sleeping in their beds.

[17]

Aeroplanes, flying in the sky, are closer to the surface of the ground than the miner is. He cannot stand up—the roof is too low. The beam from his helmet lamp is thick with coal dust. You or I would find it unpleasant enough just to *be* there; but those are the conditions in which he has to work.

The coal is cut from the face by an electric coal-cutter like the one in picture [17]. It has a big rotating cylinder with teeth round the edge. This cylinder gouges chunks of coal out of the wall and drops them on to a conveyor belt. Water is sprayed out continually to keep down the dust. The coal is carried away to the shaft. Here it is transferred into the skips that will take it to the surface.

The coal-cutter travels the whole length of the face, cutting a wide slice in the coal. When it reaches the end, it returns to carve out another strip. At the same time, the roof supports move forward automatically into the space left by the cutter. These steel pillars, which can support the thousands of tonnes of rock above them, march forward, adjusting themselves to the correct height as they go.

Miners keep all this machinery moving smoothly. They make sure that the roof supports are moving along to hold up the new roof, as you saw in picture [1]. As the supports move they leave parts of the roof unsupported, but this does not matter because work has finished there. After a while, it will collapse naturally.

As you can imagine, there is coal dust everywhere as the big cutter chops away at the face. Water is sprayed on to the coal to keep the dust down as much as possible, but the miner still gets black and grimy as he works.

A neverending task

At the end of his shift, the miner goes back to the shaft and is taken to the surface. He is tired and covered in coal dust. The first thing he does is to hand in his numbered disc, so that everyone knows he is safely out of the mine. Then he changes out of his working clothes and has a shower before going home. As he and the other miners on his shift finish work, the next team takes over.

In the modern, mechanized mine, the production of coal is a continuous process. The coal is cut, the conveyor carries it away, the supports march forward, and more of the coalface is opened up.

5 · *Other methods of mining*

Coal is not all mined by the longwall method. Most of Australia's huge deposits of lignite and bituminous coal are dug out of a huge quarry on the surface. This is called the 'opencast' method. Some mining companies in the United States use a version of the room-and-pillar system I told you about in chapter 3. Then there is retreat mining, a slightly different version of longwall mining; and a method called 'drift' mining or 'slope' mining.

When coal seams are near the surface, there is no need for shafts and tunnels. The coal can be reached by digging out the top layer of earth and rock. This earth and rock is called the 'overburden'. When the coal has been removed, the overburden is put back.

Most coal-producing countries have some opencast mines to take care of shallow seams. It is a less dangerous method than underground mining, but it tears up the countryside because everything happens on the surface.

The overburden is stripped off the coal seam by mechanical excavators. The enormous excavator in picture [18] is at work in a mine in the United States. The excavator scoops out the coal and loads it on to trucks. When the coal is all taken out, the same machine will shovel all the overburden back into place.

Opencast mining

[18]

[19] Often the coal is mined in parallel strips. First a strip the whole length of the coalfield is dug out. Then the excavator starts on the second strip, putting the overburden into the space left by the coal taken from the first strip—and so on, right across the coalfield.

Opencast mines can cover an area of many square kilometres. Therefore the collection of the cut coal can be a problem. At the Morwell mine in Victoria, Australia, the coal is carried up to the bunkers by those tremendous conveyors in picture [19].

When all the coal in the mine has been removed, the land can be used for farming, or for building upon. Within a few years, no one could know that a coal mine had been there.

Modern room-and-pillar mining

The United States has both opencast and longwall mines, but some of its deep mining is still done by the room-and-pillar method. Though modern machinery is used, this has not changed much from the original idea. Half the coal is still left behind to prop up the roof. It is a fast method of mining, however.

The coal is cut by a 'continuous miner' machine which you can see at work in picture [20]. It carves a criss-cross pattern through the coal seam, leaving the pillars behind. Then the coal is collected by another machine called a 'gathering arm loader', and taken out of the mine.

Retreat mining

Usually, longwall mining begins at the bottom of the mine shafts. The underground roadways gradually get longer as the coalfaces move further back from the shaft. Retreat mining is a version of longwall mining which is being used more and more nowadays.

[20]

[21] Two roadways are dug, one on either side of the coal seam. The roadways run from the shaft right to the far edge of the coal seam. The miners then work back towards the shaft, cutting the coal from the coalface between the tunnels.

Retreat mining is expensive to set up because the network of roadways is constructed before any coal is mined. However, one advantage of this method is that the mining company can find out whether there are faults in the coal seam before any coal is cut.

Drift or slope mines

This method is for seams very near the surface. The miners follow the seam underground, cutting sloping tunnels—drifts—as they go. The coal is brought to the surface on conveyor belts. You can see a conveyor belt on the far side of a drift mine tunnel in picture [21]. Drift mines are less expensive to set up because they do not need the winding machinery necessary in mines with vertical shafts.

6 · How coal is used

When the coal leaves the preparation plant it is ready to go to the customer. It is carried overland by train or truck. If it is being exported overseas, it is taken to the ports and loaded on to ships. The largest of these ships are called bulk carriers. Picture [22] shows coal being loaded on to a ship in Maryland. Coal is also taken by barge along rivers and canals.

Most coal is transported by rail. You have probably seen coal trains with their open trucks piled high. Sometimes a railway is built directly between a mine and a power station. At other times the railway will start from the mine but join the national railway network,

[22]

[23]

A turbine is a motor, consisting of a vaned wheel made to revolve very fast by the force of a jet of water or steam.

A generator is a machine for producing electricity, by turning mechanical energy (provided by turbines) into electrical energy.

like the coal train in picture [23].

Power stations use a huge amount of coal to produce electricity. Efficient and economical methods of transporting it are very important. To save loading and unloading time, there is a system in some countries called the 'merry-go-round'. The train goes backwards and forwards between the mine and power station, and the train is loaded and unloaded automatically without the train ever having to stop.

Coal can also be transported by pipeline, if it is mixed with water into a liquid called 'slurry'. This method is being experimented with in the United States, where coal often has to travel great distances overland. When the slurry reaches its destination, the water is removed. One coal pipeline in the United States is the Black Mesa, which runs for 450 kilometres from Arizona to Nevada.

What exactly is the coal used for at the power stations? It is simply a fuel, to power the turbines. The coal is burned beneath huge boilers. Water in these boilers is turned to steam. The steam is forced through pipes at great pressure so that it turns turbines connected to electricity generators. Some power stations use oil, but most of them burn coal.

Coal can also be used to make coal gas, though natural gas has replaced this in many countries. When coal is heated to a very high temperature in a closed oven, it gives off gas which can be burned. The solid lump left behind after the gas has been removed is called coke. Coke is used in steel-making.

Coal gases are collected, condensed into liquids, and used to make all sorts of products.

One valuable part of condensed gas is coal tar. Coal tar can be separated into pitch and oils. The pitch is used to make water-proofing materials like asphalt and roofing. The oils are used for plastics, cosmetics, and medicines.

The by-products of coal gases include chemicals, disinfectants, soaps, fertilizers, paints, and moisture-proof building materials.

Then, of course, coal is burned in the home. It is burned under boilers which supply hot water and central heating. It is also burned in the grate, to provide the kind of cheerful atmosphere you see in picture [24]. Some homes have solid fuel cookers which cook the food, heat the water, and keep the kitchen warm, all at the same time.

In many countries people have to use smokeless fuels, to cut down air pollution. Anthracite is a naturally smokeless fuel. Other types of coal can be turned into smokeless fuels.

When you think about all these uses of coal, you can see why we are taking it out of the ground so fast. The trouble is that, like all the world's harvest, coal is unique. When we have used it all up, whatever shall we replace it with? I try to answer that question in another book in The World's Harvest series—*Energy from Sun, Wind, and Tide*.

[24]

Index

anthracite 8, 31
Arizona 30
Australia 7, 9, 25, 26

bell pits 14
bituminous coal 7–8, 25
Black Mesa pipeline 30
Britain 9, 21

cage 18, 22
cannel 8
carbon 6–7
China 9
coal
   amount mined each year 9
   amount still in the earth 10, 13
   constituents 6
   cutting 16, 23–4
   early discoveries 8–9
   formation 5–8, 12
   gases 30–31
   tar 31
   trains 20, 29–30
   types 7–8
   under the seabed 12–13
coalface 16, 22, 27
coke 30
computers 13, 16, 18
continuous mixer 27
conveyor belts 22, 23, 26, 28
core samples 12, 13

drift mines 28
drilling 12–13
drill ships 13

electricity production 10, 30

fossils found in coal 5

gathering arm loader 27
geologists 11–12
Germany 9

lignite 7, 25
longwall mining 15, 21–4, 27, 27–8

Maryland 29
methane gas 16, 22
mines
   ownership 21
   roof supports in 24
   size of 20, 26
   types of
     bell pits 14
     drift 28
     longwall 15, 21–4, 27
     opencast 25–6, 27
     retreat 27–8
     room-and-pillar 14–15, 27
     slope 28
mining
   early mining 9, 16
   mining companies 11–12
   offshore 12
Morwell mine, Victoria 26

Nevada 30

opencast mining 25–6, 27
outcrops 8–9

peat 5–6, 7
pipelines 30
pit ponies 16
pits, *see* mines, mining
Poland 9
power stations 10, 29, 30
preparation plant 18–20, 29

retreat mining 27–8
roof bolting 17
room-and-pillar mining 14–15, 27
Russia 9

safety down the mine 21–2, 24
seams
   depth 7, 17
   formation 5–6
   thickness 7
seismic surveys 11, 12
shafts 15, 17, 18
shift work 21, 24
slope mines 28
slurry 30
surface work 18

turbines 30

United States 9, 17, 21, 25, 27, 29, 30

Victoria 26

winding gear 18, 20, 28
working conditions 22

Acknowledgements for photographs: Australian Information Services, picture on title verso and nos. 2 and 4; British Rail, no. 23; Central Electricity Generating Board, no. 6; National Coal Association, USA, nos. 13, 20, and 22; National Coal Board, U.K., picture on cover and nos. 1, 3, 5, 7, 8, 9, 10, 11, 12, 14, 15, 16, 17, 18, 21, and 24; State Electricity Commission of Victoria, picture on title page and no. 19.